Rafig Y. Aliyev

EUROPE WITHOUT CAPITALISM

political and philosophic thoughts

Order this book online at www.trafford.com
or email orders@trafford.com

Most Trafford titles are also available at major online book retailers.

Typing and computer design: N. Aliyeva
Translated by: A. Aliyeva

11 Vagif Ave. AZ1007, Baku, Azerbaijan
Tel./fax: (994 12) 441 01 32/33/34
E-mail: aliyevrafig@gmail.com
WWW.RALIYEV.AZ

Printed in the United States of America.

ISBN: 978-1-4669-9279-5 (sc)
ISBN: 978-1-4669-9278-8 (e)

Trafford rev. 04/23/2013

www.trafford.com

North America & international
toll-free: 1 888 232 4444 (USA & Canada)
phone: 250 383 6864 • fax: 812 355 4082

The book brings forward the author's personal attitudes to the analysis of the present difficult political, economic and financial situation in the EU member states. It reveals the author's prognoses of the necessity of system reforms, avoiding useless attempts to reanimate the obsolete political and financial structure of capitalism. In the author's opinion, for objective reasons, modern capitalism is not able to solve problems of preservation of life supporting financial institutions the European states and the West are facing today. The author thinks that Europe has to go over to a post-capitalistic way of development. This is the call of the times, the demand of the historical moment. Capitalism as a system of political and economic development has completed its historical mission having brought western countries to the highest level of economic and technical development, creation of the best welfare for the countries of Europe and the West, i.e. it has exhausted resources for progress. Principally, new empires should have been built 10 years ago, i.e. it was time for Imperialism. However, today it is impossible for objective reasons.

Countries like China, Russia, former USSR republics and part of the third world will develop according to the capitalistic way of development, taking into consideration a mass of mistake the West has made. They have a huge amount of resources for capitalistic way of development.

What will happen to Europe in future? Prof. Rafig Y. Aliyev has specific proposals about that worthy of attention and discussion. However, the delay of important decisions on the very political and financial system may turn into a tragedy for many nations, including the EU member states.

The book is meant for a wide circle of readers.

CONTENTS

TO THE READER

It is more than evident that the construction of the European empire, started in the early 1960s, has failed.

For quite obvious reasons, mainly political ones, the supposed empire remained a closed system, not having enough strength for self-preservation, let alone expansion and struggle with its enemies, rivals in economy, building of efficient army and, of course, consolidated variant of external policy.

All this has gradually led to degradation of the idea of united Europe.

The idea did not turn into the ideology for all Europeans, presenting titled nations, claiming to be the best. Local nationalism became a serious handicap to implementation of general European policy and forming of supranational European ideology. All this came to grief. Nowadays, there are no conditions to reanimate the idea.

Nationalistic moods driven inside as a result of Germany's defeat in World War II have found the way out under conditions of liberal democracy.

Truly, I cannot understand the essence of the word combination.

It turns out that there is democracy, leaving no space for freedom, i.e. liberalism. It is nonsense.

Nevertheless, liberal democrats run the show in the European area, rather the name is not significant for them.

The main thing is more freedom, more indifference and more connivance as necessary conditions for establishing economic and legal chaos. This is my view of Americans' and Europeans' liberal economy today.

Suffice it to remember that the idea of establishing the union of European states, the sort of "the United States of Europe", appeared as early as the beginning of the XX century. Almost 60 years ago, the attempt to revive it was made, but it has not been implemented even 50 percent.

For this reason at least, the European politicians' and optimists' persistence and their desire to create a strong united Europe, the European empire as a matter of fact, are groundless and was such 10-20 years ago, too. The ground, on the contrary, became fluid and turned into a green bog, into which the economically and financially weak European states are gradually plunging.

The course of the events of recent ten years, i.e. constant lower growth rate and decrease of European states' living standards convince us that not a EU member state will be able to come through unscathed from the increasing bog. Little time is left to make a decision. ***Europe is under time pressure.***

The Europeans are gradually losing their instincts of self-preservation, self-control. They try not to cause panic and, apparently, think that European lucid minds will save them within the present system.

This is rather not to lose hope for recovering suddenly. The Europeans try "not to give a horse the bridle", to rely upon a miracle because of such double state.

In such conditions sluggishness and hesitation may mix with the feelings of a wild mad beast. For, even a polecat driven into a corner defends itself desperately and may turn into an unbridled beast.

Nobody will be able to avoid thunderbolts, to hide behind a tree hoping to avoid strong peals of thunder—people's anger, force, which cannot be measured by present ultrasensitive nano-devices.

The Tsunami in Japan compared with people's anger will seem to be harmless prank of nature.

People's anger contains everything: fire, water and the strength of powerful volcanoes and hurricanes.

This is proved by the history of revolutions in Europe, tsar's Russia and in present Afro-Arab states.

Not to see and to understand this is tantamount to a crime against nations, people and, of course, closely related world community. The responsibility is very great and suspicion is strong . . .

Every person understands what it presents in his/her own way, but, of course, hardly remains indifferent. Since it can become a reality for his state in future.

People in modern Europe are unable to defend themselves and fight against the financial crisis alone.

This would be contradictory to Europeans' delicate classic taste and would discredit the status of European standards preserved till now. ***One weapon is left—intellect. The Europeans have it enough.*** *Why then do problems have pressure on European pragmatic intellect and prevent them from defending themselves? Europe deserves the best!*

This is my wish to them and the incentive of writing the article.

P.S. The contents of the book in Russian and English were presented to the public in late 2010—early 2011.

Rafig Y.Aliyev

NEW EUROPE WITHOUT CAPITALISM

This important problem has been spinning like an invisible plane over European politicians' heads for recent decades, and the distant between the earth and it is decreasing. Figuratively, landing needs a space purified of obstructive elements. The airfield is the whole territory of Europe. This matter is very serious and complicated. The destiny of the Europeans and those in close relation with them depends on the solution of the problem in the direct sense of the word. Therefore, the whole world, every person, even hundreds of Somali children, dying of hunger every day, are interested in Europe's choice of a new way of political, economic, financial and moral development.

Recently all serious politicians, economists and analysts of different states and international organizations have acknowledged that European economy, based on the principles of liberal market relations, has been in deep crisis . . . There are no prerequisites for optimism. European politicians are becoming petty before the very eyes of the world community; moral values are degrading, more and more states and nations, not only European ones, are falling into extreme poverty and unemployment. Nobody has managed to stop or, at least, to slow down the regress yet. At that, active and hasty searches for ways out of the hardest financial crisis lead to a deadlock every time, and the European researchers— politicians and philosophers cannot come upon the tracks of 'casual factors', leading to such a state so far. The method of study of the deplorable situation of the political, economic, financial and moral component of the European Union (27 EU member-states) tells upon inadequate political and economic decisions.

The overall analysis of the present situation in EU member states demonstrates that one very important circumstance—*the fact that the growth of further successful development of capitalism in European countries has stopped*—is not taken into consideration while the reasons of European nations' misfortunes are studied and explained. Capitalism has reached the finishing tape 'successfully'. Therefore, all decisions made without considering and understanding this main factor are not for European nations' good. First of all, the matter requires system changes, not palliative restoration or reanimation actions. In its present unhealthy state, the capitalistic way of development, taking into account, first of all, the interests of banks, exchanges and political forces cannot offer the European peoples more than has been done. The resources of this system of government of economy, finances and social environment have been depleted. The reanimation of capitalism or Americans' favorite *liberal economy* turns into an unsolvable problem. For these obvious reasons, some politicians and analysts start surmising that the system of state government should be changed.

I am sure that the present political system in the West should go down in history as an important but completed stage of human evolution.

As the events of recent five-ten years show, various attempts to expand possibilities of capitalism further development will be no success for a banal reason: *the immunity of capitalism has weakened*. Therefore, I do not get into details of such a natural state of one of the social and political system like capitalism. I will do it in other articles or, maybe, in open disputes, dialogues, discussions. The most important thing today is that it is necessary that other variants of replacement of the outdated system of capitalistic relations should be found and examined taking into consideration the fact that capitalism *has completed* its lofty, historical mission.

It is important to notice that it did this with dignity having brought the European and US states to the peak of scientific and technical development.

Like any living being, every system has limits of development and existence, figuratively, the expiry date. The same was during slaveholding and feudal systems. Capitalism has them, too.

Without taking into consideration this main and conceptually important fundamental factor, we will not find the worthy and only righteous answer to the question: *how to take the European states to safe areas, to take them out from the mouth of the dying dragon, into which modern capitalism in developed states has been transformed?*

Like any object or a historical moment, capitalism in Europe has lived out its term, and its end is inevitable. The birth and death are the law of nature, progenitress of all living beings and all communities. We should let the European capitalism leave the historical arena in Europe and the USA with dignity, say, without applying the principles of euthanasia (compulsory easy death), without rough shoves and pushes to the stomach. It can successfully continue in the states like China, India, Russia and post-Soviet states, which need capitalism, but, of course, taking into account the mistakes of the European states and US.

Today, Europe and the USA must find a new system of further social, economic and political development for their own sake and for those who are much behind Europe in their development but in close relation with it. This transitory stage is a historical exam for present Europe, the motherland of many revolutions, innovations, approbation of political, social and economic development systems. It has neither moral nor legal right to fail the exam or to subject the European nations to long-lasting suffering and extreme violence by stopping the world's development. Like Libya, Europe needs the Transition Council to be helped by the world civilization. First of all, it is European peoples' welfare and peaceful future that depends on the results of the work of the transition council of the kind.

New Europe can and must present the world community *a communication map of successful and peaceful isolation from classic capitalism*. All the states of the world are

interested in the successful fulfilment of this important project, for this is the only way Europe can remain among leading developed states and preserve its status quo.

Most scientists and political figures believe that nowadays western states, the USA and Europe in particular, are not the engine of the world development, but, on the contrary, the inhibitor of the world financial and economic system; they do not let feel independence from players (*pay attention: not employees but players*) of world exchanges, who often colluded, have an adverse effect on pricing of such strategic goods like oil and gas, gold, capital issues, large enterprises shares, thus undermining, in the direct sense of the word, the world's financial system and destroying the aggregate of world trade rules. Virtually, they hold in their hand the 'tail' of a big unhealthy dinosaur which is the world financial system in its present state, in my view.

Radical, fundamental changes in political, economic, and financial spheres are necessary to go to a new, more qualitative level of development and to save the states of developed capitalism. Naturally, they will be of revolutionary nature. Neither a European state nor the USA is able to avoid this destiny. Changes are inevitable. This is not only the call of the times, but also vital necessity, a matter of life and death. The destinies of millions of Europeans are at stake. And not only of Europeans . . .

I do not have the slightest doubt that these changes will take place soon. The matter is only the time and forms of radical changes. According to my initial analysis, there are two variants at the minimum:

First. Changes are taking place at the level of supreme power in the states of capitalism and are gradual, transparent and irreversible. Strong political and state figures are needy to share historical responsibility and to announce these aims, to convince peoples of necessity of construction of *'post-capitalism'*—a new, unprecedented community. I understand that in the present strained neurologic and psychological situation it is difficult to the Europeans to live another year or two with a new hope for something new. However, the fear of ***what*** expects them if they refuse to make radical, revolutionary changes which are not popular today will help them be patient and render assistance to those who will light the torch of 'the post-capitalistic community'. The price of saving Europe from social calamities is very high, but the thing is worth its while.

Second. Synchronically, social outbursts are happening nearly in all the states of Europe, and the masses destroy every obstacle on the way of a normal, self-sufficient and steady life. At this undesired variant, both power and people lose in political, economic and financial respects. Instead, Europe will have an uncontrollable chaos in all the spheres of life. The black cloud of social outbursts will cover the sky over many states and will poison the Old World—residents of common motherland of most world revolutions. As a result, western peoples, always relying on power (or force of the monarch, king), will remain without guidelines like hungry wolves in a desert, and, naturally, they will be ready to fight to survive. Europe will plunge into the abyss of local wars and divide into small states.

I would like to propose the following as the explanation of the above given variants:

Exchanges, turned into gamble play areas, might remain and function but as a part of financial and economic life of the states of the world financial space. We know that the virtuality of play at exchanges is one of the main reasons of the world financial crisis, the collapse of world currencies—dollar and euro.

However, the exchanges should act as a real mediator: goods—money—goods plus modest interest. Principally, there should not be unreal, virtual and illiquid financial operations.

The world community should prohibit 'gambling' (there is no other word for this) at exchanges. The reality of present time should manage the exchanges spared by new conditions.

Banks. This sector of the financial system is important for preserving and insuring citizens' cash resources and for issuing loans for development of medium and small businesses. As a matter of fact, the system should change substantially. Banks should not be the sources of immense profits by using available methods which allow bankers robbing investors. The shareholders and bank owners should not grow rich as they do today. Actually, these are crimes shielded by bankers and political powers. Banks should be like savings banks of the Soviet time with some substantial changes and taking into account necessities of the time. The bank leaders should stop illegal transactions, as a result of which a group of people become billionaires without exerting efforts, but, to put it mildly, resorting to swindle and illegal turnover of plenty of money. The system of financial exchange and money laundering must be excluded from banking system as well as different international financial funds like the International Monetary Fund (IMF). For example, the IMF Director is an ordinary average citizen, but as a leader of the international semi-mafia-controlled organization he grows rich very soon. It is impossible to become a billionaire, even receiving a high salary. So, the conclusion is evident.

The political system. The above-listed will become impossible if the political system of state government is not changed. A lot of innovations should be done in this sphere. Here, many innovations are needy. The 'democratic' way of electing leaders of states and parliaments should be given up; the party affiliation system should be liquidated and their functions should be completely handed over to trade unions. In this case, unlike an ordinary party member, who is only needed at elections, every member of the trade union will be constantly interested in qualitative state and society government. ***This is a cornerstone in the cause of saving Europe from forthcoming destructive wars. As a structure of capitalism, parties should stop existing together with capitalism.*** Without parties and their political shady transactions, it will be easy to establish justice in a new European society and to provide more or less real distribution of the wealth of the state, to

provide peoples' balanced equality, to give them a chance of living beyond constant lie, slander and ideological war of power-loving people, based on own parties. The principle of society division in two, or even three groups like 'friends, strangers and the so-called 'homeless" in the sense of 'nonpartisan' will disappear then.

The list could be spun out and grounded theoretically and practically. The afore-said is the basis of radical changes, the first important statement of the question of saving Europe.

The main thing is how much Europe is ready to accept the reality and irreversibility of radical change of the present system of state government, real peaceful settlement of people's relations in society. The life without capitalistic postulates of development is the call of the times Europe, the USA and we live in. You should collect your thoughts and understand real and true reasons, present state of economy and finances of your states without fearing the difficulty of solving problems of transition from capitalism to more just society.

I am sure that Europe and the USA have no other options of further successful development.

Nevertheless, the righteousness of the above given suppositions, prognoses and analysis results may make all of us, till the end of this year or the mid of the next year, not only think over what to do, but also over why the historical chance to save Europe from a great deal of difficult problems of capitalism overgrowth has been missed, the capitalism which has been at stagnation for several years.

I would like to point out that the above has nothing common with fantasy. This is my worded idea waiting for its implementation. I am ready to persist in my opinion at any level, before any audience.

Everybody knows that every cause starts with an idea that follows fantasy. However, today's Europeans have no time for fantasy. The matter is very serious, grandiloquently, supremely important. Having missed this historical chance and, to all appearance, the only one, Europe will pass a sentence upon itself and will execute it itself.

It would be naïve to think that some of high politicians, economists and financiers want to commit suicide. To say the truth, 'suicide' is not far off, it is just necessary to see its outlines and to feel the breath of the wind from this terrible composition—swift flight up and decline that led to the financial and moral crisis, real destruction of everything done for centuries.

To preserve basic elements of the historical past and present, the Europeans should, first of all, have strength of will, acknowledge irreversibility of burying European capitalism. This is natural death, and it is not shameful. All living beings are to die one day. There are many lucid minds and pragmatists in Europe. They are able to find a way to the brains of single EU members, politicians, busy, mainly, with financial bags mending, to explain people the purposelessness of hard work on pulling European states out of the mire. The life buoy has been thrown down into the European mire, widening day by day.

The number of those wishing to catch at the buoy may be more than we can suppose, and drowning men's only desire will be to come up to the surface of turbid water.

Figuratively, in this case the capitalistic states' population will need heaven and space just 'to pray, with their hands up, and to ask heavenly powers to help them to overcome the inevitable transition period from capitalism to fairer society less painfully, to give them will and wisdom to see and to endure agonizing separation with the previous system of interrelations and states government courageously, and, of course, to give them strength to rejoice at a new, happier mode of life, new interrelations without ruling part of party leaders, billionaires, mafia-controlled intercontinental cartels, and at new distribution of state wealth'.

However, the fear of delusion and indecision of new reforms may bring European nations to big losses and tragedy. They will witness involuntarily a full collapse of their habitual mode of life they created for many years.

Life accompanied by fallen morality observed today will seem to them to be street

boys' pranks. They will not care of morality and consciousness then. Every European will be only occupied with saving their life and life of their relatives and friends.

High morality, European democracy with its numerous vices will not be able to stop the process of degradation of society which the plug was pulled on and the spirit of which has been let out. Only dreamers will hope for its return, since such a crazy idea may not come into the mind of a person of considerable intelligence, all the more, be good for their states.

THE THIRD WAY IS THE OLD EUROPEAN MODEL

The European nations' patience to be tested

I would like to express my attitude to the events happening in present Europe more specifically, as a reply to the readers' numerous e-appeals.

There are, of course, diffirent opinions, approaches and political and financial prognoses about the nearest future of EU states which are in the thick of political, economic, social and financial shocks.

Despite this, I would like to dwell on the main aspect of ***what*** has led old Europe to the deep financial, political and social crisis without going into details of the whole set of reasons of the present crisis of many faces.

Some readers think the content of my previous articles to be true and corresponding to the present situation in Europe. Others believe that the financial crisis in Europe is not related to the state of economy in the USA, where capitalism develops differently. Some others ask the question: 'What does the European capitalism differ from the American capitalism?'

Principally, all the readers are right. There are no exact answers to the questions, though there should be.

We understand that there are cause-effect relations of any event, including the situation in Europe, the reasons of which are quite specific and historically grounded.

One thing is left: to find out and to submit to the readers' consideration the most important reasons, to try to go back to the time when and how Europe's social and economic development started after World War II and what Europe has reached today. Then we will understand the reason of the present deep financial crisis. Naturally, my previous article *New Europe Without Capitalism* does not consider this comprehensive problem. It just reflects the statement of the problem. However, as a matter of fact, the European capitalism that became the main idea of creating the European Union in the early 60s of the last century differed much from the American model of capitalism. It had both the political and economic hidden motive. *The idea of the European Union should be based on rules and laws of development and establishment of a new society, which would have been at* ***an equal distance from capitalism and socialism.***

The researchers of Western Europe's political history know that this way of development was then called hybrid, i.e. a certain synthesis of two social and political system of evolution; the hybrid should have been attractive to the rest of the world (basic regulations of the synthesis of the kind took their places in the development of Yugoslavia in B. Tito's time).

In those times the left movement in western European states was stronger than others. The defeat of fascism and a new geopolitical situation in the European continent changed cardinally the political and economic system of whole Europe. To stop the spread of the idea of socialism and to impede the appearance of new foci of revolutions, the European political groups set forth the idea of 'the third way' of development in the zone outside the USSR's influence.

Against this background, historically unprofitable for Eurocentrists, there appeared variants of the establishment of the European Union. However, analyzing the events of those times, we can conclude that, as a matter of fact, they managed to slow down the rapid rate of left forces and to weaken their positions in society for a while by such political maneuver not foreseen beforehand. But there are still many left parties with similar programs of the population social defense, growth of the state role in the financial and economic sphere.

However, after World War II restoration works required much time and many efforts. It took years to form and implement the new idea; the following events in the USSR, especially after the replacement of the political leadership in the mid 1950s gave impetus to the final option of the system of European states administration in favor of the rich, technocrats and multimillionaires.

The slogans of social defense and just distribution were moved to the background. 'The third way' was gradually removed from the agenda of the European Union. All the mechanisms and forms of society and state development were 'adjusted' to the Procrustean bed of the so-called European democracy. They were characterized as certain universal euro-standards in economy, politics and civil society we all know well.

However, the rapid and unexpected refuse from the first model, more social and more profitable for society, and gradual swift growth of economy as well as the inability to use personal success within European laws adopted in a hurry led the idea of full

liberalization of the financial market to failure and the population's social security to infringement.

As the final result, Europe, being closely related to the world financial system, the dominant of which is the USA, reached the present political and social and financial crisis as a part of the state prior to the universal financial collapse.

Nevertheless, strange as it may seem, the third way did not sink into the oblivion. In the early 1960s, it was suggested to the states of Arab East and Africa, which were hence called the states of 'the third world'. That is, they were suggested the very way during the realization of which the first European social model experienced failure.

The reason is simple: the then level of development of these states was very different from that of the European states, and they were not ready for such high standards and changes in the social, political and financial fields. The western states 'helped' them with the failure of the model for political reasons not to let the influence of the communistic ideology grow in the Arab-African political field. It was then that the first radical religious movements like 'The Muslim Brotherhood' in Egypt were created.

However, back to the European affairs, it should be mentioned that the idea of the European model was approximately the following:

1. *The European social model directed at the acceleration of the role of the state, increase of social costs, workers' legal defense and just distribution and regulation.*

This was a partial copy of the model that worked after World War II in the Soviet Union and the states of Eastern Europe, and, naturally, was a serious moving away from the pre-war capitalistic way of development of the USA and Europe;

2. *The liberal social model, according to which reduction of state expenses for social programs, uncontrolled free labor market and absence of clear-cut state distribution were dominant.*

This kind of model was also an innovation for Europe where development was slow and conservatism in all the spheres of life was strong. Nevertheless, this social program was successfully used in the Anglo-Saxon world of those times.

Finally, Great Britain's EC membership played a fateful role. The ruling elite, rich citizens and large owners supported the idea. It was close to the American model based on the liberal economy and the state's scanty role in solution of social, economic and financial problems. It placed the state's role in social defense of human labor at a low level: the salary minimum (the matter is the European standards), high taxes and absence of legislative restrictions, a chance of growing rich for the rich Europeans.

Today Europe, both Western and Eastern, has become a hostage of the mistaken selection of the second model of development the promotion limit of which has ended too soon, and the growth of the European capitalism has stopped. Spiteful tongues say that the present space of Europe is not enough for the development of the model. And it is impossible to create an empire by colonizing other states.

Therefore, Europe has been 'feverish' for 10 years. The situation is difficult: to go out from the crisis, the previous model should be rejected, the exchange and banks system should be reformed and cardinal changes should be made in policy or the rich should be made to share their gain.

Such cardinal changes require strong political will, corresponding conditions and, of course, not less strong and sagacious politicians, economists and financiers. Europe has all the conditions. The matter is another thing: present political and financial and economic institutions in Europe are not ready for such changes. Therefore, the conservatism and the rich Europeans' unwillingness to part with the conditions and sources making big 'non-labor' profits are the main, if not crucial, obstacle on the way of overcoming of the crisis. Besides, any serious reforms require much time, and the European political and financial elite do not simply have it. Years are needed to reform the system of interrelation in society—between government and citizens.

For this reason apparently 'major repairs' or 'restructuring' of Europe or, roughly speaking, 'mending' of financial holes in the European space, are beyond present European politicians' and state figures' power. For this banal but main reason, unfortunately, the social outburst is gaining strength, and we will soon witness the undesired beginning of serious hard times when our European friends' patience is tested . . .

P.S. *I have deliberately ruled out in my article the way out from the crisis by means of involving European nations in regional wars. I am based on the historical experience that 'politicians wage wars to retain the power when they cannot do anything worthy at peace'.*

POWER FROM WEAKNESS

One who cannot negotiate another way raises his fists. As expected from logic of the events of recent 5-6 years, European states have started imitating their politicians showing anger, committing pogroms, arsons and outrage upon human dignity.

The world witnesses that the solution of problems by means of force has become popular and cool according to people preferring to reach their ends by all means. What is more, it has repercussions, effect and draws attention of press, local and foreign parliamentarians, active international organizations, known for endless preoccupation, etc.

Unfortunately, an overwhelming majority of participants of such 'activities' suffer as a result of methods accompanied with the use of force, police truncheons, tear-gas, rubber bullets, in some cases—guns.

Only some people achieve fame, which is sad in itself and vulgar by form.

Nevertheless, there are followers of the fame of the kind, though this kind of scandalous fame should be categorized as 'a bad name'. In other words, this fame is due to the loss of dignity or innocent people's life, the fame that will not bring true joy.

The historical principle is one and the same; it has not changed for centuries: "you want to be famous, say goodbye to honesty, or more specifically, to honor and conscience".

This is so in most cases, though there are exceptions—history and nations never forget true heroes.

You know that people are very different and their perception of the surroundings, events assessment and conclusions are different, too.

It should be observed that 'creation of a problem and its solution by means of force' has been turning into a norm of everyday life in most developed countries as if there is no alternative, or problems cannot be solved peacefully, even the simplest problems like a legal approach to all citizens, i.e. in accordance with legislation.

I realize that we all were created with potential good and evil, love and hatred, compassion and indifference, and therefore, each of them can only become apparent under favorable conditions. The article is about Europe, where, in my view, the destiny of the whole world is at stake figuratively.

The 10-year history of the political and economic development of the world, especially, Europe, indicates that some representatives of the European establishment aspire to achieve visible, but doubtful and vicious fame. The process occurs together with a rapid growth of science, technology, telecommunications; this commands true respect, since all this becomes a desired pastime in some states of Europe. For example, in France, Germany, Spain, Italy, England, etc . . . The aspiration to the vicious fame is the result of excessive use of force instead of the mind, what is inherent in classic Europe. This is sometimes at the cost of deprivation of liberty or even life, sometimes dignity and human honor, or killing many people. The negative happens, mainly, to unemployed people, deprived of successful future . . . The representatives of the category of 'unhappy' people are the youth of the state and the emigrants from underdeveloped states of Africa, South-East Asia and India.

According to some European analysts, this may happen as a result of understanding the absence of any prospect of keeping stable social, economic, political and cultural development of great states which have a dozen of social problems pending solution. It becomes obvious that most developed states do not have finances and other 'peaceful' means. In addition, according to western mass media and decisions of the supreme power, there is no political will of the leaders who were nearly always farmed out to ambitions and corruption of transnational and global scale.

Therefore, both powerful state and weak, unemployed groups of people play the same bloody game in accordance with their abilities and with the tools they have.

The scenario of these 'games' is unchangeable; for example, pogroms, arsons as a trenchant argument of implementation of spontaneous or intended aims and giving vent to accumulated negative emotions, hatred, spite and open injustice, corruption in the higher power echelons.

Pogroms and arsons in France, England, Germany, Spain and Greece differ little from each other. At times, the executors define their motives of bellicose behavior differently, each in their own way.

For example, these illegal, criminal in itself, actions in Germany are carried out by Neo Nazis, in France and Great Britain—by emigrants, in Greece—by ordinary people, whose money is taken by united EU financial structures and the International Monetary

Fund in the direct meaning of the word, turning their purses and pockets inside out.

Naturally, pogrom-makers in the number of cities of Europe are no match for their skilful politicians who, besides other wealth and resources, have powerful military force they use against people in their country and abroad.

The rules of fire and death game are different. Say, everybody ought to do his own thing. Everybody has what he/she can do at the moment and uses it in full . . . Actually, there are no serious restrictions and obstacles on part of the UNO Security Council and other powerful international organizations.

This is felt both in the selection of the means and the process and results. A complicated but possible partial combination of motives of those who make pogroms and plunder gives politicians a chance to think, to make conclusions that the population in their cities do not follow their democratic way not because of good life.

On the contrary, people started imitating their authorities in everything related to the use of force, as if compensating the lack of finances to improve living standards of the population, which has to pay for politicians' mistakes. Apparently, they do not know what to do in difficult circumstances. The powers that be cannot separate good and evil in this complicated problem and choose between antagonistic qualities yet. They have not found an acceptable way out yet.

Meanwhile, we ask questions about what, principally, the events happening in European cities differ in from NATO's actions in Africa, Iraq, Libya, and Afghanistan, where the use of force became the only argumentation in negotiations. They, too, destroy, burn, kill, and plunder the peoples of the countries for no reason, without explaining anything to their people, the world community, which has unnoticeably cultivated a complete indifference to the world events.

Apparently, everybody is busy with his own problems and do not take care of other people's misfortunes as it used to be 20-30 years ago.

I am sure that the world is expecting the realization of the foresight of the classics of the late

XIX-early XX centuries about the development of capitalism and coming of a new era—the era of magnificent funeral, and the beginning of a fairer, more humane life, new human and just rules of co-habitation in the post-capitalistic system of political values, including moral, social, political and economic ones.

However, I would not like the funeral to be organized by the same pogrom-makers, pillagers and gangsters. In capitalistic states there are well-organized trade unions which will probably shoulder the responsibility of historical mission to govern the transition period from decaying capitalism to socially just society, moving away all political parties and armed bands.

I am the first to accept this 'transition council' as the only legitimate body representing the population of these states. This is not a trick on the extraordinary French President Nicolas Sarkozy who, despite all principles of law, was the first to accept the so-called Libyan rebels' 'transition council' that had not been established yet. We are not alike; I take everything more seriously.

Indeed, I am sure that this kind of scenario of the end of capitalism and the beginning of the new era of the world development would be convenient to the absolute majority of mankind. The capitalism has done its historical mission. Nobody should doubt this.

Analyzing the events of the recent 2-3 years, it should be concluded that the tragedy of big and developed capitalistic states of the present time is not in their deviation from the Western democracy they have announced, from the system of social justice, but, in my view, in the fact that they forgot to define the limits of their 'greatness', their abilities and stopped seeing, feeling and taking into consideration the vital interests of other states and nations. This leads or has led to a gradual decrease of these states' prestige, to financial, economic, military and cultural degradation. Europe has reached a blind alley. This will rather result in the collapse of the ugly system of capitalism in the states of the Old World.

I have no doubt that everything comes to that. Capitalism, like any other social

and political system of state government, requires, besides other things, definite clear-cut guidelines of, personal space to leave the limits of which is dangerous. However, the modern European capitalism and its apologists neglected the rules, carrying out invasions to other states and nations, having decided who and how should govern one or another state, how to live and work, which God to believe and worship.

Unfortunately, they have taken the path of serious bad luck, large misfortunes; in a simple word, they have reached the terminus, without leaving an alternate route. Mass losses in wars had a ruinous influence on the inside situation in these states, the living standards of which are going down; there have been revealed obvious facts concealed from the population and world community for years, according to which the very 'great' powers turned out to be not so great but simple states living at the expenses of debts and credits, and the leaderships of the states cannot pay their people due salaries, pensions, and to settle accounts with foreign creditors. The pride and greatness are gradually turning into shameful deeds requiring repentance before the people of their states.

This, too, requires a great strength of will: not every person can confess his failure. Judging by the reaction of many high-ranking officials of European states, at the moment they are practically unable to tell their people the truth that they have not been able to restrict themselves to what they had for many years. They wished to do their best, but it turned out to be deplorable as usual. If we add that they may take responsibility for the present problems up on themselves, I cannot prognosticate the Europeans' behavior, though they are ready to let people try their leaders for hardship and suffering.

The events of recent 7 months indicate that European nations have lost optimism about self-sufficiency of liberal values for further successful development. Unfortunately, the European nations do not have a real alternative to rotten capitalism. They have not thought about the alternative up today. The course of events has taken them by surprise.

Back to the main point about the destiny of capitalism in Europe, I would like to notice that if the idea of necessity of government change in the states of the world capitalism is obtained and used by semi-literate, unbridled and unorganized youth in England, France, Germany, the global tragedy will be inevitable. Personally, 'the Spain's Indignant movement', trade union movements in Greece and other EU states impress me.

They could lead the transition stage from outdated capitalism to community of social justice and people's equality, could give the population of these states a chance to feel dignity, pride and joy of living in these really great states, to give them a hope for future, which is covered with a thick dark fog so far.

The aggressive behavior of the English youth suggests that in the country like England there are many destitute people without amenities, young people deprived of future; this is, in fact, the indication of ugly form of social and economic development in recent 10-15 years; the absence of widely-advertized democratic and liberal values and freedoms that have been destroyed; more or less valuable fragments have been passed to rich members of society who still believe that most politicians defend their interests.

"Everything is done for the sake of money, to live somehow, not to die of hunger . . .". The words of one of the pogrom-makers in London mean much, and do not require mass arrests—over 1,300 men for three days (even B. Assad's army in Syria the West hates cannot put so many people under arrest). Prime Minister David Cameron stated with inadequate aggression inherent in him about severe punishment of juvenile 'pogrom-makers' not specifying the fact that it would be useful to eradicate the reasons and motives of citizens' such extreme actions.

The use of force is the last argument of the power and it may only aggravate the situation and will cause new tides of unrest and aggressiveness on part of the youth who has nothing to lose. Despite the young Englishmen's attempts to resemble their politicians, there are too many differences between leading politicians and unemployed

youth, making pogroms and committing arsons.

There is only one way out: the system has become obsolete and led European and western population to the desired, historically foreseen boundary at which, apparently, the power should be peacefully passed to ones who are worthy of leading Europe along the new path—the path of establishment of community of social justice. We would not like the process to be bloody.

"TO INFECT THE WORLD WITH HATE!"

The Neo Nazi and Ultra Nazi terrifying antihuman slogan is hovering as a black kite not only over Europe. It aspires to be global, universal like "Scoundrel of all the countries, unite!" Let us, potential victims of the world rabble, unite, too! For, unfortunately, time is on their side so far.

Every person comes to an opinion sooner or later that people created their world, certain dogmas, codes of conduct and friendship, and drawn a circle, to leave the limits of which means to violate the rules of co-existence. We shaped and filled the world the way we like and according to our imagination and related everything with the will of God, the Master of celestial powers.

The history of human appearance and evolution proves that not a person would be able to live with the peace of mind without dogmata, framed with human belief in the existence of the beyond.

The fact that we attach some divinity to the world we created has not been proved yet.

This was not proved scientifically and many of religious dogmata remain the mystery; the people have reconciled to this long ago, taking this for granted.

Nevertheless, common people's many deeds are often outside the permitted limits.

Only then we start clarifying whether these deeds are related to unknown mysteries of celestial powers which control our actions.

Not having found trustworthy answers which would confirm our surmises, we estimate man's deeds from different viewpoints, minimizing the divine influence with statements like *The person got crazy, It's the devil's work, He is mentally incompetent, in the state of affect.*

We refuse to believe in what is obvious at that. Man has the freedom of actions; only earthly circumstances, his real physical and mental state, attitude to the world and his place in it can influence his choice.

The unexpected deeds of some members of society are often related to the fertile ground (the social ground is meant) on which, due to people's indifference and egoism, there is a tall tree, in the shadow of which everybody has a rest. At that, we do not pay attention to how the tree has grown and why it fans with cool everybody, including scoundrel terrorists, coming to the tree and the people in its shadow with sinister intentions and hate. Time shows that different groups of interests are organized under the tree which are sometimes directed at the extension of the area of hate, spite and even murder and death of society and the very tree.

The reality of these scenarios is proved by the swift growth of nationalistic movements in Great Britain, France, Denmark, Germany and Norway where a well-known tragedy took place on July 22, 2011. It killed 76 people and undermined the hope of millions of Europeans, who created illusions of the reliability of European peoples' security system.

Unfortunately, Ultranationalism and Neonazism have rooted themselves in the European ground; therefore, it will be difficult to root them out or to neutralize their consequences by legal and political means. In addition, it is obvious that it is not enough to resort to severe administrative sanctions, to block the financial flow nourishing the ultranationalists in order to influence these double threats.

The situation is aggravated with the fact that under the tree of evil, grown into the European community, there appeared a worm in its depth—Religious Radical Extremism, which does not annihilate the roots of Ultranationalism and Neonazism in Europe as many people think naively. On the contrary, they nourish each other, getting along with each other.

As a result, the danger of the ominous triad "Religious extremism—Ultrantionalism—Neonazism" for society increases manyfold.

There are no supranational religions in Europe like in the East. Therefore, the triad of the kind, in other words, triple threat for European community is not only possible here, and it is already real. There is no antidote for this sinister combination or real ban on it either in religions, or democratic laws, sometimes countenancing the relaxedness under the pretext of the free expression of will.

Many experts believe quite reasonably that the alliance of the kind may only reinforce the ultranationalists', neonazis' and religious extremists' potential.

It should be mentioned for justice' sake that, except Islam, nearly all the religions are in good "business" relations with nations and nationalistic movements.

According to Islam, not a nation is privileged, in simply terms, there is no one 'in charge'; everything is focused upon Allah.

Some religions—Buddhism, Judaism, Christianity and Gregorian branch as the first heretic sect in Christianity, according to historical data, are national. It is not clear what content prevails in them—religious or national. This thought is corroborated by a lot of examples.

The study of radical nationalists' and neonazis' behavior indicates that supporting their behavior with religious attributes, they are satisfied with their hate and hostility towards ones they consider 'the enemies' of their nation and religion which they are supposed to protect and through which they get divine blessings. However, Religious radicalist hardly wishes to sacrifice himself for the name of the nation or religion for what he would become posthumously 'an honored' nationalist or 'national hero' or 'a martyr'.

No, heroic deeds are not typical for ultranationalist, neonazi or religious radical despite religious 'tattoos' all over their clear-shaven heads. In that case, they may deprive themselves of a chance to enjoy other people's humiliation, death; this is the final aim of nationalism of many faces as a whole—to be superior to others, the master of destinies.

According to the European mass media, allegedly, the young monster from Norway Anders Behring Breivik put on the earphones not to listen to music when he shot dozens of people on the island ("What a low European finesse" Friedrich Nietzsche would say), but not to hear his victims' cries and moans that could influence him and prevent him from completing his 'cause', to avoid noise and to kill as many people as possible, as though only mentally incompetent person can do this.

Those who try to characterize his deed as the action of a mentally incompetent person are just insincere deliberately. They are criminally mistaken, grounding his desire to stop up his ears with the state of his psychical health.

Those who do not want to accept the presence of Christian Super-Extremism in some of European states think this way. But, following formal logic, Breivik should have closed his eyes, too, not to see the nightmare he created in the pious country. He has not expressed regrets of what he did up today.

Many politicians try to whitewash their faces blushed with worries and shame as well as their power and, of course, religion

the benevolence of which they need for political ends, trying to get points. For this, they are trying by all means to incline public opinion to accept what happened simply as a tragic incident, as unexpected bolt from the European democratic blue, which hit the wrong address—stable, peaceful, successful democratic Norway.

The people of Norway deserve the sincerest sympathy and compassion. They have hard times today and, therefore, turn the drama insignificant in comparison with the events in Libya, Iraq and Afghanistan into the tragedy of the European scale. It is really a terrifying tragedy for the victims' friends and relatives.

I understand this. I sympathize with them and I am ready to compassionate together with those whose relatives were killed by the bustard and villain, European religious fundamentalist, Neo Nazi and ultranationalist.

At the same time, I know that the world is one and interrelated. This commits us not to think only about our own welfare. There is folk's saying: *'Good never comes out of evil'*.

Politicians should take this into consideration when, behind the successful people's back, decide to send soldiers to take part in wars against innocent people, during which tragedy, death, humiliation and human sufferings happen. They say that one boomerang is enough to awaken indifferent conscience. Of course, if it is not lost in the quantity of personal material and financial interests.

This is unlikely and I do not believe in this. However, this is the subject for another talk . . .

Nevertheless, history will keep the truth about the present events.

It is generally known that history is often not clear till the end, not correctly interpreted or presented.

This is the reason of the following mistakes which, increasing in number, destroy the foundation of the house—the very history rewritten without scruple for centuries. Thus, according to the French historian Marc Ferro, the author of *How the Past is Taught to Children,* who studied and wrote about the history of different nations, "today nearly every nation has several histories, superimposing and confronting each other.

Naturally, everybody does this in accordance with their interests".

Nowadays, history is rewritten by many people in the West, including Europe, and the East.

As a matter of fact, this has no relation to real history. I am sure that history has always been and will remain the object of political speculations.

Misrepresenting the history of our days again and again, many US and European politicians try to make people look at everything from the strangely formed unknown American and European point of view.

According to their actions, outside these artificially imagined 'historical tales' they see threats for themselves. This does not allow them seeing the world widely and taking into consideration 'the form, structure' of the eyes and faces of other nations and states.

Since the 'point' in the context of European view is very narrow and covers just some fragment of the viewed space, according to the laws of Physics, the European view of everything and everybody changes very rapidly and only in the zone of initially defined limits, restricted by tasks in the interest of the world capital.

Many nations of the world, especially developing ones, are not ready for this kind of variant, I would say, to cosmic velocity of development. They see no clear-cut scope in the viewed space yet; they are free in motions, actions. They have not formulated the means of their growth and cannot prognosticate their future. All this is in future.

Therefore, time they have does not fetter them, does not restrict them to certain traditional canons, international conventions and laws. They resist the western influence the way they can—roughly, clumsily, illogically.

Maybe, for this reason, Radical Nationalism in European states together with Religious Extremism, Ultranationalism and Neonazism, pass into neurosis, a hard-to-cure disease.

The latter, it is apparently neurosis of many faces, is not thoroughly studied

by psychologists and neuropathologists worldwide.

The reason is simple: like in case with cancer, here, too, we do not understand the essence of the phenomenon. Religious Extremism in combination with Ultranationalism and Neonazism is a very complicated phenomenon; to fight it will be difficult, too.

In such cases psychoanalysts would say that the process occurs in parallel with gradual change of human consciousness, in which it is consolidated.

Therefore, the history of mankind provides a great deal of evidence that it is impossible to deprive man of the mind at one stroke. He dies slowly, painfully until the process is a doubtful 'success', and man loses it forever.

The same happens with faith. It comes faster than mind develops. The faith, uncontrolled by the mind for a long time, often manages to mature and brings the mind to suicide, capturing the threats of control over the believer's deeds, leading him to reclusion, martyrdom or terror and state of a suicide bomber.

This picture is well known—the cult of martyrdom in Christianity, Sufism and reclusion in Islam, Religious Fanaticism-based acts of terror in different parts of the world, like, for example, in the neoreligious sect Aum Shinrikyo (currently known as Aleph) in Japan.

We have to establish the fact that, unfortunately, a major part of independent states, including post-Soviet republics, have been experiencing the transition period. They are in certain virtuality—between a long religious and political stagnation that came to an end and a rapid religious revival and growth of the two important elements of life (politics and religion, or in terms of philosophy, matter and consciousness). The deep analysis of the recent events indicates that both the factors are burdened with the wrong interpretation of the essence of being, of the life of an ordinary person who, unfortunately, does not want to live without a false hope for eternal life, estimating his miserable existence in this unjust world where

most people think themselves to be not other than a helpless nonentity.

At once Africa appears before the eyes unwillingly: Niger, Somali, Ethiopia and a major part of the outlying districts of the modern civilization.

This means that we ought to keep to certain rules of living, reminding us that nowadays any deviation from good should be regarded as a motion towards evil. This obliges us, as people, community, not to allow our social ground being favorable for growing the tree of national extremism and religious fanaticism.

I dare to note that the above said refers mainly to the West, particularly to Europe, where the trees with noxious fruits on them are ages-old.

The fruits of evil and hate may envenom the whole Europe where capitalism has reached a deadlock.

While Europe and we are mourning for the people killed in the Norwegian island, NATO's soldiers, say, many young *Anders Breiviks,* are killing tens and hundreds of people in various regions of the world, and the European and world 'democratic free' mass media are keeping silent about that. The papers and TV channels of the so-called civilized states do not speak about, or misrepresent evident facts about human tragedies in the states, where the NATO soldiers and aviation, including, unfortunately, Norwegian soldiers, too, are coolly shooting peaceful populations, humiliating killed young women, prisoners in Iraq, Afghanistan and Guantanamo.

The whole world knows that Norwegian Air Forces, together with British, French and American fighters and bombers are still bombing Libyan cities, civil facilities—hospitals, schools, TV buildings, the sovereign state leader's palaces. Tens, hundreds of peaceful people, including old men, women and children, patients at hospitals, are killed.

Unfortunately, the prospering Europeans, in this case the people of Norway do not have compassion upon and protest against all this.

Is not this cynicism? Is this fair, legal, and, finally, is not this sanctimony before their own people and the world nations, among which there are ones persecuted, humiliated, victims of political intrigues and ones, called 'inviolable' among people, who should be 'protected' and mourned for for a long time and need luxurious funeral?

I think the latter is necessary for everybody dying of gangsters', extremists' and combatants' bullets.

All are equal before death. We cannot change this rule of life. The same should be during the life, too. Everybody knows that every action causes resistance and everything has consequences for which people should be responsible morally and legally.

As a matter of fact, the world's present events are the infringement of weak people's rights, humiliation of whole nations, states, killing of hundreds of thousands of people outside Europe and the USA, UN's connivance as well as indulgence to the wars in the Middle East, Africa, transnational drug barons' luxurious life, appearance of new millionaires and billionaires as a result of open robbery, impunity and injustice and nearly absolute absence of responsibility for crimes against mankind.

They are wars in Palestine, Iraq, Afghanistan, the former Yugoslavia, the tragedy in Nagorno Karabagh and Azerbaijan's 7 occupied regions and in many states of the world.

Is not this the sound of the alarm of calamity for all the people of the world? What else evidence is necessary for the world community to set the bloody war makers thinking and acting in accordance with their conscience, Christianity—with love to man without distinction as to nationality, religion or state he lives in?

However, I have to point out that despite the SOS signal, broadcasted uninterruptedly, people have got used to it . . .

It is a bad criminal habit. Anyway, it should not replace our human nature. We must prevent those infecting the world with hate by all means.

This is my viewpoint as a citizen, my moral credo, the impulse of inner anxiety of my ***'Ego'*** . . .

www.ingramcontent.com/pod-product-compliance
Lightning Source LLC
Chambersburg PA
CBHW021247280526
45784CB00005B/2261

9781466992795